D0341553

Praise for *The Meaning* by Steve Taylor

"Insightful and delightful, Steve Taylor's poems are like a beautiful mist of champagne bubbles on a background of infinite space and silence."

— CATHERINE INGRAM, author of *Passionate Presence*

Praise for *The Fall* by Steve Taylor

"One of the most notable books of the first years of this century, and I am convinced it will be one of the most important books of the whole of this century."

— *INTERNATIONAL JOURNAL OF TRANSPERSONAL STUDIES*

"An important and fascinating book about the origin, history and impending demise of the ego — humanity's collective dysfunction. *The Fall* is highly readable and enlightening, as the author's acute mind is at all times imbued with the higher faculty of spiritual awareness."

— ECKHART TOLLE, author of *The Power of Now*

Praise for *Waking from Sleep* by Steve Taylor

"The most enlightening book about enlightenment I have ever read."

— ERVIN LASZLO, author of *Science and the Akashic Field*

Praise for *Out of the Darkness* by Steve Taylor

"A fascinating and illuminating journey through the landscape of spiritual transformation."

— SHARON SALZBERG, author of *Loving-Kindness*

"*Out of the Darkness* is filled with amazing stories of enlightenment brought about by life's most difficult circumstances.... A truly inspiring book!"

— SUSAN JEFFERS, PhD, author of
Feel the Fear and Do It Anyway

"Steve Taylor reminds readers of the resilience of our human spirit and our capacity to find light in the darkness as we pass through that dark night of the soul to find a brighter dawn."

— DAN MILLMAN, author of *Way of the Peaceful Warrior*
and *The Four Purposes of Life*

"A wonderfully clear and inspiring book about the way great suffering and ordeal can lead to sudden awakening. Its importance for our menacing times and for the transformation being birthed by them cannot be exaggerated."

— ANDREW HARVEY, author of
The Hope: A Guide to Sacred Activism

Praise for *Back to Sanity* by Steve Taylor

"A book with a massive scope which opens our eyes to a new way of understanding the world, and is also a pleasure to read."

— CHRISTOPHER RYAN, author of
the *New York Times* bestseller *Sex at Dawn*

"Insightful, confronting and liberating.... I recommend Steve Taylor's brilliant new book to everyone. It is destined to be a modern classic."

— ROBERT HOLDEN, PhD, author of *Shift Happens!*

An Eckhart Tolle Edition
www.eckharttolle.com

 New World Library
14 Pamaron Way
Novato, California 94949

Copyright © 2015 by Steve Taylor

Text design by Megan Colman

Library of Congress Cataloging-in-Publication Data
Taylor, Steve, date.
The calm center : reflections and meditations for spiritual awakening / Steve Taylor ; selected and introduction by Eckhart Tolle.
    pages   cm. — (An Eckhart Tolle edition)
ISBN 978-1-60868-330-7 (hardback) — ISBN 978-1-60868-331-4
(ebook)
1. Spiritual life. 2. Meditation. I. Tolle, Eckhart, date. II. Title.
BL624.T394 2015
04'.32—dc23   2014046887

First printing, May 2015
ISBN 978-1-60868-330-7
Printed in Canada on 100% postconsumer-waste recycled paper

 New World Library is proud to be a Gold Certified
Environmentally Responsible Publisher. Publisher
certification awarded by Green Press Initiative.
www.greenpressinitiative.org

10   9   8   7   6   5   4   3   2   1

5660 9117
5/15

THE CALM CENTER

*Reflections and Meditations
for Spiritual Awakening*

STEVE TAYLOR

Selected and introduced by ECKHART TOLLE

• An Eckhart Tolle Edition •

New World Library
Novato, California

Also by Steve Taylor

THE CALM CENTER

Not I, not I, but the wind that blows through me!...

Oh, for the wonder that bubbles into my soul,
I would be a good fountain, a good well-head,
Would blur no whisper, spoil no expression.

> — D. H. Lawrence,
> "Song of a Man Who Has Come Through"

Contents

Introduction

How religious you are depends on the nature and strength of your beliefs and how deeply you are self-identified with them. How spiritual you are depends on your degree of presence in everyday life, which is to say your state of consciousness.

The essence of all spirituality is presence, a state of consciousness that transcends thinking. There is a space behind and in between your thoughts and emotions. When you become aware of that space, you are present, and you realize that your personal history, which consists of thought, is not your true identity and is not the essence of who you are. What is that space, that inner spaciousness? It is stillness, the calm center. It is pure consciousness, the transcendent I AM that becomes aware of itself. The Buddha called it *sunyata*, emptiness. It is the "kingdom of heaven" that Jesus pointed to, which is within you, here and now.

As presence increasingly arises within you,

it manifests in many different ways: inner peace, empathy, an outflow of goodwill toward your fellow human beings, creativity, a heightened sense of aliveness, freedom from dysfunctional and compulsive thinking, a deep appreciation of the present moment. All these shifts and many other changes greatly enhance the quality of your life.

Presence can also empower and inspire the spoken and written word. All true spiritual teachings use words as pointers toward that transcendent dimension of consciousness that is presence. In some mysterious way, the words that arise out of presence are imbued with a certain power that goes beyond their informational value and is reflective of presence. That power can awaken or deepen the presence in those people who listen to or read those words. All true spiritual books have that power. You can, and indeed will want to, return to and reread them many times, because a certain shift in consciousness happens within you as you read. You enter the state of presence.

The Calm Center is one of those rare books. It belongs to the genre of poetry, which has been recognized since ancient times as a highly appropriate medium for the expression and transmission of spiritual truth. Many ancient scriptures can be considered either as poetry or as existing on the borderline between poetry and prose. The Upanishads, the Bhagavad Gita, the Dhammapada, and the Tao Te Ching are all poetic in nature. In these texts, meaning, images, sound, and rhythm interact to create a harmonious whole whose transformative power is activated in the consciousness of the reader or listener. Then there are the great mystical poets of Sufism, such as Hafiz, Rumi, Kabir, and Attar; and the Buddhist poets Basho and Milarepa. In the Christian tradition also there are great mystical poets, such as St. John of the Cross, Angelus Silesius, and of course Meister Eckhart, whose writings, with their masterful use of images and metaphors, could be described as poetic prose. In more recent times, the spiritual dimension is present in the works of numerous poets, such as Wordsworth, Whitman, Rilke, and many others.

Steve Taylor's *The Calm Center* is a contemporary incarnation of that ancient tradition of poetic spiritual discourse. The ultimate subject matter of almost each one of these poems is the reader's state of consciousness. If you open yourself to their transformative power, and read slowly and attentively, then you will find that each piece will work its magic within you and bring about a subtle but distinct shift in your state of consciousness. It will free you from the mental noise of compulsive thinking and raise you into the alert inner stillness that is presence. It will awaken you to the spiritual dimension. And if you enjoy reading these poems repeatedly, their cumulative effect will be potentially life-changing.

I recommend that you keep a copy of the book on your bedside table and another at your place of work to provide spiritual sustenance during your breaks, however short. The reading of each piece can become a mini-meditation, and often one will be all you need at any given time. I have read some of Steve Taylor's poems out loud to the participants at spiritual retreats, where they were enthusiastically received. I would advise that you also occasionally share your favorite pieces aloud with your partner, spouse, family members, or group of friends. You, as well as those who listen, will benefit greatly from this, as will the quality of your relationship. Just make sure, however, that the other person is open and receptive, so that you don't cast these pearls before people who are too unconscious to appreciate them.

Allow me to start off your spiritual reading pleasure with this little excerpt from a poem:

I wish I could show you,
When you are lonely or in darkness,

The Astonishing Light

Of your own Being!*

This little gem certainly does not look out of place in the pages of this book. It was written, however, over six hundred years ago by the great Persian Sufi poet Hafiz, who was given the epithet "Tongue of the Invisible" — which goes to show that words that emanate from presence are timeless.

— Eckhart Tolle, author of
The Power of Now and *A New Earth*

---

* Hafiz, "My Brilliant Image," *I Heard God Laughing: Poems of Hope and Joy*, trans. Daniel Ladinsky (New York: Penguin, 2006), 7.

The Only Place

When the future is full of dread
and the past is full of regret
where can you take refuge except in the present?

When maelstroms of tormenting thoughts
push back the barricades of your sanity
the present is the calm center where you can rest.

And slowly, as you rest there,
the niggling thoughts and fears dissolve
like shadows shrinking under the midday sun
until you don't need refuge anymore.

The present is the only place
where there is no thought-created pain.

The present is the only place.

The Challenge

How will you know how strong you are
unless your strength is tested?

How will you know how deep you are
unless turmoil breaks your surface
and forces you to dive?

How will you know what sleeps inside
until the whole of you is challenged to wake
    up?

Then you'll turn inside to gather your
    resources
your untapped reserves of strength and skill
then rise like a sun, amazed by your own
    brightness,
stronger than you ever suspected
deeper than you ever dreamed.

Divine Dissatisfaction
(The Opening)

When you sense there's something more
when the life that used to satisfy you no longer
    seems enough
and security seems suffocating and pleasures
    lose their taste
when dreams of success don't motivate you
    anymore
and diversions don't seem to divert you
when familiarity seems oppressive, like a coat
    that's too old and tight,
and every repetition of the old routine
makes you feel more stale and weary

When you find yourself aching
with a sadness that doesn't seem to have a
    source
with a hunger that seems too subtle to satisfy
when strange energies are pulsing through you
like the tremors of an earthquake deep down
    inside
and you can feel the ground shifting
and are afraid of losing balance

and you ask yourself, "What's wrong with me?
Why can't I be happy anymore?"

Have no fear — there's nothing wrong with
    you.
This isn't anxiety or depression,
it's divine dissatisfaction.
You're not breaking down but breaking
    through.

This is your awakening
the tearing of the veil
the opening of your soul.
Your real self is emerging, slowly, painfully,
through the hard skin of your chrysalis.

The old world is receding behind you
and you're waiting at the threshold of the new,
    disoriented,
wondering how to make sense of this strange
    place.
But as long as you have the courage to move
    forward
a guide will appear and your path will form
    before you
and a glorious adventure will begin.

And soon the lushness of this landscape won't
    startle you anymore
soon the brilliance of this sun won't dazzle you
soon the vastness of this space won't feel
    overwhelming
and the magic and meaning of this new world
    will embrace you.

Become the Sky

This cage you've been trapped inside
for longer than you can remember
might seem so sturdy and secure
that you don't even dream of escaping
    anymore
like a bird that used to beat its wings
but now just lets them hang limply by its sides.

But the bars of your cage aren't solid.
They're a mirage made up of fears and desires
projected by your restless mind
fueled by the attention you give them.

Just for a moment let your mind be quiet
and see how fears evaporate
see how desires withdraw
like the claws of an animal that's no longer
    threatened.

Watch the bars melt away
and let the world immerse you.

Let your mind-space merge with the space out
    there
until there is only space without distinction —
stretch your wings and become the sky.

The Voice inside Your Head

One day you'll grow fed up with the voice
    inside your head
with its constant murmurings of discontent
its fearmongering thoughts of the future
and its questioning of every choice you make.

One day you'll turn to it and calmly say, "I
    refuse to listen"
then stand back and look away
turning your attention to your surroundings
or to a quietness and spaciousness you can
    sense
inside you, just behind the voice.

The voice is so self-absorbed
that at first it won't even notice it's being
    ignored
and will carry on chattering away to itself.
You'll still hear its complaints and criticisms
but they won't convince you anymore —
you'll doubt them, laugh at them, reject them.

And gradually, without the fuel of your
    attention,
the voice will become more hesitant
will stumble and slow down, leaving space;

until eventually that self-assertive drawl that
　　demanded to be heard
and seemed to submerge the rest of reality
will be no louder than a whisper, like a gentle
　　breeze
that seems to be part of silence.

The Core

It can take a whole lifetime to become
    yourself —
years of feeling adrift and alone
acting in a role you were never meant to play
stammering in a language you weren't meant to
    speak
wearing clothes that don't fit
trying to pass yourself off as normal
but always feeling clumsy and unnatural
like a stranger pretending to be at home
knowing that everyone can sense your
    strangeness
and resents you because they know you don't
    belong.

But slowly, through years of exploration,
you see landmarks that you recognize
hear vague whispers that seem to make sense
strangely familiar words, as if you had spoken
    them yourself,
and ideas that resonate deep down, as if you
    already knew them.
And slowly your confidence grows
and you walk faster, sensing the right direction,
feeling the magnetic pull of home.

And now you begin to excavate
to peel away the layers of conditioning
to shed the skins of your flimsy false self
to discard those habits and desires that you
    absorbed
until you reach the solid rock beneath
the shining molten core of you.

And now there's no more uncertainty —
your path is clear, your course is fixed.
This bedrock of your being is so firm and
    stable
that there's no need for acceptance
no fear of exclusion or ridicule.
Everything you do is right and true
deep and whole with authenticity.

But don't stop. This is only the halfway
    point —
maybe even just the beginning.

Once you've reached the core
keep exploring but more subtly
keep excavating but more delicately
and you'll keep unearthing new layers, finding
    new depths,
until you reach the point that is no point
where the core dissolves
and the solid rock melts like ice

and the self loses its boundary
and expands to encompass the whole.

A self even stronger and truer
because it's no self at all.

A self you had to find
so that you could lose it.

The Secrets

You can't grasp at the secrets
prize them from the earth
or pluck them from the air.
The harder you try to hold them
the more they lose their form
until they leak away.

You can grind matter down to the tiniest grains
until it collapses into nothing
but its essence will always elude you.
You can pin nature down and torture her
but she'll never tell you what she knows.

You can't use force or even effort —
you can only create the right conditions
reverse the beam of your attention
and make a sacred space inside.

Let your mind become as empty as a cloudless
     sky
and as calm as the surface of a lake
until your depths are rich with stillness
and the channel is wide and clear enough
for the secrets to flow through
and reveal themselves to you.

The Story

Your story is always there
if you need to remind yourself of who you are
like a stream flowing beside you
that you can always step into and swim with for
    a while
whenever you lose direction or feel vulnerable
and need to refresh your sense of self.

And when you're flowing with that stream of
    memories
you might feel proud of how far you've come
to this moment of bright achievement
look back upstream and smile with vindication
at the fools who slighted and doubted you.

Or you might ache inside with failure
looking back at the meandering muddy tracks
that haven't led anywhere
except to this place of pain.

You can be a hero or a villain, depending on
    your story.

Or you can let the stream flow by
and accept this moment in its wholeness
without reference to any other, before or after.

You can sit and observe, outside the story,
not as a character but as the author
grounded in another identity
that was never created
and doesn't need a plot or conclusion
because it's already complete.

The Alchemy of Attention

When a mist of multiplying thoughts fills your
    mind
associations spinning endlessly
images jostling and memories whirling
free-falling through your inner space
you can always bring yourself back to now.

This morning, making breakfast for the kids,
I catch myself daydreaming and with a gentle
    mental nudge
remind myself of where I am.
And straight away the kitchen clutter turns into
    spacious presence —
a mosaic of sunlit squares across the floor
fading and brightening with the passing clouds
the metal rims of stools firing sparks
steam-curls floating over cups
reflecting silver spoons
the perfect stillness of spilt coffee grains
the gaudy yellow and blue of detergent bottles
and the window smudges exposed by sun —
everything perfectly still and real
everything perfectly itself.

Attention is an alchemy
that turns dullness to beauty
and anxiety to ease.

The Spiritual Teacher

"You can't find happiness in the world," the
    teacher said.
"It's a place of imperfection. That's why it's
    full of suffering.
You have to go beyond it, into the realm of
    spirit.
That is where fulfillment lies."

There was an otherworldly glow in his eyes
as if he was from another dimension
too ethereal for the earth
just visiting, with no desire to stay.

"The body is a husk, nothing more," he
    continued.
"A temporary vehicle for the soul.
And the more you indulge its desires
the weaker the spirit grows."

I left the meeting and wandered the streets,
    looking at the sky.
I walked through the park, along the
    promenade,
underneath the swaying branches of the trees.

And I felt spirit speaking
through the quiet sentience of the trees
through the gentle murmurs of the wind
through the hissing and swelling of the sea
through the smooth soft flowing of the clouds.

Every blade of grass, every wave of the sea,
every cloud, every stone, every particle of air
glowed with its own consciousness
subtly sentient, quietly alive,
always there but at a secret frequency
beyond the normal spectrum of awareness.

I felt the awesome power of spirit
pouring through and pervading the world.
I opened myself up, I let the power embrace me
and became part of the communion too
my whole body tingling and sparkling with
      spirit.

And I never saw the teacher again.

The Shock

There are so many ways to feel dissatisfied
so many different needs to meet
so many goals to keep striving toward
so many problems to try to fix
so much of the past you wish you could change
so many fears about the future.

No wonder you feel overwhelmed
like a traveler carrying too many bags
with too many paths to choose from
who has to keep stopping to rest
until he can't go on, and collapses.

How could you ever be happy?
Life's too demanding and complicated.

But then — the shock of an illness or an
    accident.
Death creeps behind you and swipes you hard
    across your back
awakening you from your torpor.
Suddenly the fog dissolves
and you can see the narrow ledge you're
    walking
— the one you've always been walking —
    between life and death.

And now it's all so simple and makes perfect
    sense —
life is temporary and fragile, precious beyond
    measure,
and life contains nothing except this present
    moment
this beautiful bright river of experience.

And suddenly those needs stop niggling at you
the guilt and fear stop gnawing
the phantoms of the past can't scare you
    anymore
there's nothing to worry about or to be
    afraid of.

Everything obliterated
but the glory of this moment
and the grandeur of the world itself.
And you know that this is all there is
that this is where fulfillment lies
and everything else is only a shadow play of
    the mind.

The Light
(from Different Lamps)

I saw the light burst across the sky
like a flower opening behind the clouds
and the whole world was flushed with harmony
shimmering like the sea at dawn.

I saw the light glow inside my mind
seeping through the darkness of inner space
at a certain point of stillness
like a pool of pure white water.

I saw the light shine through my baby's
    eyes —
two crystals gleaming with unconditional love
straight from the universe's golden core.
All-emanating, all-embracing — the light of
    light itself.

The Mask

Don't make yourself a mask to meet the world
a mask that plays your life so well
that's so affable and entertaining
that you're always the center of attention —
a mask you can't let slip, even for a second,
in case your real self shows through
and the audience realizes that they've been
    tricked
and their affection turns to ridicule.

The mask makes life easier —
there's a storm of impressions, thoughts, and
    feelings
that could confuse and overwhelm you
but you can stand firm, with the mask
    protecting you,
reflecting back the world like a cold metallic
    shield
deflecting any pain that comes your way.

And it's easier still when you don't stand back
    and watch anymore
when you become the role you're playing
and forget you were ever anyone else.

But the mask is like a child that never grows up
that will never be self-sufficient;

you have to keep feeding it with attention
and make sure it never meets silence or
    solitude —
the two predators that threaten it.

And eventually the mask will crumble
when you can't keep up the effort anymore
and collapse like an exhausted parent at the end
    of the day.

Then your real self will stumble free
stunned after such a long imprisonment
dazzled by the brightness of the sun
reeling from life's complexity
naked and open to terror and delight.

And the world will trust you
the human race will welcome you
and slowly others will unmask themselves
    around you
as you feel yourself connecting to a deep
    nourishing flow
beyond the fragile separateness of masks —
the richness of your being, opening
to the richness of others' beings, and of life
    itself
the wholeness of your being opening
to the wholeness of life itself.

When Problems Seem
to Lie Ahead

When problems seem to lie ahead
don't rush forward to meet them
as if they're long-lost friends —
let them lie there, let them wait.

Let them sleep until it's time to meet
then give them due attention
resolve them as best you can
then go on your way, leaving them there
without ever looking back.

Or even, when the appointment comes,
you might find yourself waiting, waiting,
    waiting
until you realize that you've been tricked
that there was never a problem and there's
    nothing here
except a long thin shadow, cast by your
    thoughts.

The Struggle

The struggle never seems to stop —
you think the last wave's washed over you
and at last you can relax
let your guard down and look around
but already there's a new wave
rising and rolling toward you.
So you sigh and steel yourself for pain
and suffering shivers through your bones
    again.

The Buddha wasn't wrong —
life is a dark rainbow
with a million different shades of suffering:
trauma coiled so tight inside your mind
that you can't locate it, let alone release it;
failures reverberating from the past
dread of the future unfolding
self-defeating thoughts too ingrained to
    dislodge
neurons misfiring, hormones rising,
nerve endings exposed or agitated;
too many demands like hungry children
screaming for attention;
too many different streams of information
bombarding and cluttering your brain.

Contentment is an uneasy truce
a precarious balance that always breaks.

But sometimes there's a moment between the
    waves
when time splits open like an atom
and suddenly you're floating beyond sorrow
part of a brilliant mosaic of meaning
that makes anxiety seem impossible.
A blazing symphony of harmony
and you're completely attuned, participating —
the harmony is you, and playing through you.

And even though you have to come down
    again
each time the waves lose a little strength
the suffering grows less substantial, lighter,
    and thinner
like a ghost you can almost see through.

The Pressure to Do

The pressure to do never stops
even when your schedule is empty, with every
    loose end tied up,
even when you've guided every project to
    completion
and know you've earned the right to relax
and relish your achievements, at least for a
    while —
but the pressure won't let you rest.

The pressure is never satisfied
like an animal with an endless appetite
that devours every activity then hunts for
    more.
It's with you as soon as you wake up
and keeps nagging and nudging throughout the
    day
and sometimes keeps you awake at night
whispering, "There's still so much to do,"
reminding you of what you didn't manage to
    do today
and what waits to be done tomorrow.

The pressure to do convinces you
that all this activity is necessary
that the present only exists to serve the future

that moments are empty spaces that must be
    filled
that time is an enemy and your life a constant
    battle
and every achievement — even every
    completed task — a tiny victory.

But you don't have to let the pressure push
    you —
maybe you've done enough already.
Maybe there's nothing more to do
apart from what is necessary.
Maybe further achievements
will only dilute what you've already done.

Stand firm and resist the impulse
stand back and let the momentum fade.
Relax and let the pressure pass you by
then guide yourself gently back to a standstill
like a train that slows and finally comes to rest.

Then your life will open up like a landscape all
    around you
and time will expand until there is no time at all
only free-flowing unbroken space.

Then the pressure to do will give way
to the ease and grace of being.

The Fall

Sometimes there's a space between thoughts
when a trail of association winds to an end
and the mind stops for a moment
scanning for a new story to spin —
just a tiny gap, a millimeter wide,
but you might find yourself falling between the
    thoughts
as if between the rungs of a ladder
afraid at first, waiting to crash against the
    ground,
until you realize there is no ground.

You can sense the endless empty space below
but there's no anxiety, no vertigo —
you're not falling but floating
beyond the reach of gravity
an astronaut of inner space.

Relax and let yourself be cradled
amazed by the immensity of your being
beyond your brain and body
stretching everywhere without reaching
floating everywhere without moving
being without identity.

The Sea

It feels so right stepping into the sea
returning to the source of life
walking into a lover's arms
and melting into oneness.

Wave after wave, relentless,
pulverizing and kissing me
freezing, swelling mountain ranges
snowcapped, avalanching, lashing.

Like an enlightened being, the sea stills the
    mind
silencing everything in its roar
shrinking problems into insignificance
and thoughts to distant whispers.

In the sea all opposites collapse —
Ice-cold lava that spits and simmers
whiplash waves that gently stroke
a roar of perfect stillness.

And I can feel its sentience
the cold caress of a living being
a creature that swells over the skin of the earth
breathing in and out.

Space

Without space there is no music, only
    discordant noise.
Without space there is no language, only
    meaningless sound.
Space weaves patterns of meaning
breathes order into chaos
holds structures together, with the harmony of
    form.

And without space life is meaningless too —
a roar of constant activity
so crowded with demands that you lose
    perspective
so cluttered with responsibilities that you lose
    direction
and finally lose yourself.

But when space pervades your life
shapes begin to form, patterns start to emerge,
and your vision becomes clearer, against an
    empty background,
and you can sense your purpose again, and
    return to your path.

And when space pervades your being
the discord inside you begins to heal, the chaos
    begins to clear,
as if a river of ease is flowing through you.
You feel yourself emptying and expanding
until you're vast and whole but limitless
and the vastness of your being is full
of harmony and meaning.

The Smile

At the moment of brutal disappointment
when you realize that your hopes were illusions
and you're ashamed of your gullibility
and angry with the world for stringing you
    along
for letting this foolish game go on so long
and your future seems bleak and stark
without those filters of delusion
and you survey the wreckage of your life
wondering if you were ever who you thought
    you were —

Maybe you can sense a part of you
that's not a part of this
that's standing outside this psychic storm
untouched by the chaos
peering through the rubble and the clouds of
    dust
looking on and smiling —
knowing that this damage is only superficial,
just to your facade, not your foundation,
and that when the debris is cleared away
there will be more space inside
for your essence to shine through.

There Is No Need

There's no need to surround yourself with
    luxury
to treat yourself to the best of everything
metallic fridges and designer bags
the colors of the season, the car of the year,
to show others that you're special.

You don't need daily doses of good news
to lift your mood when you feel glum.
You don't need compliments or presents
or flirtatious smiles across the room
to keep you happy with yourself
or hourly fixes of pleasure
to set your brain cells jingling.

There's no need to say the right thing
to be charming or funny or stylish
so that strangers notice you, and your friends
    still like you.
There's no need to pretend, or to prove
    yourself.
You don't need the respect of others
in order to respect yourself.

There's no need to cover up the silence
with the chatter of radios and TVs.

There's no need to fill the empty space
with jobs that don't need doing
or words that have no meaning
or tasks that have no purpose
except to fill the empty space.

You only need to meet yourself
to let the discord within you fade away
and find the stillness underneath
the place where you're already whole
where there is no need to seek or strive
because there is no need.

A Moment without Thought

A moment without thought
and the background noise ceases
and I can suddenly hear
the silence between sounds
the silence beneath sound
from which all sounds emerge
like waves from the sea.

A moment without thought
and the fog disperses
and the world is filled
with translucent light
new dimensions of detail
and sharpness and color and depth.

A moment without thought
and these suburban streets
are a pristine new world
like a garden glistening with dew
the morning after creation
as if a husk of familiarity
has cracked and fallen away
leaving naked primal is-ness.

A moment without thought
and I'm no longer standing separate

no longer an island but part of the sea
no longer a static center
but part of the flowing stream.

A moment without thought
and the train has stopped between stations
and there was never any motion, never any
    track.
A moment like a wormhole
infinitely expanding
like stepping through a narrow gate
to find an endless open plain —
the panorama of the present.

And this new world of no-thought
is neither alien nor unfamiliar
but a place where benevolence blows through
    the air
and soft shimmering energy fills every space
and the sunlight is the translucent white light
    of spirit.
The deepest, closest, warmest place —
the ground where I am rooted.

You Don't Have to Think

You don't have to think.
You don't need to anticipate before you act
and provide a running commentary while
    you're acting
then replay your actions afterward
at the same time as watching and criticizing
the actions of others.

You don't have to argue with yourself
about events that dissolved away decades ago
or resurrect ancient humiliations
that can still inflame you with hurt and hatred.
You don't have to weave imaginary worlds
where you can satisfy your secret desires.

You don't have to watch helplessly from the
    side
while your mind whirls away
creating unnecessary discord
and wasting precious energy.

You don't have to think
except when thought is necessary
when you need to bring your conscious mind
    to bear
to deliberate, analyze, or organize

or to let your imagination drift
allowing ideas and insights to emerge
from the undercurrents of your consciousness.

Thought should be a tool
we can pick up when needed, then lay down
    again,
leaving us undisturbed.

Otherwise there is no need for thought
to disturb the natural stillness of your mind
to dilute the purity of experience
to distort reality through interpretation
to confuse the present with the past
and interfere with the impulses that gently flow
from the silent part of you, which knows
better than you think you do.

Time to Stop Striving

It's time to stop striving
to stop hurtling forward like a blinkered horse.
It's time to stop pushing,
like a mad-eyed explorer who won't admit
    defeat
convinced the only reason he can't forge ahead
is that he's not trying hard enough.

It's time to give up
the endless struggle to become
and accept that this is all there is
that there's nothing more to gain or lose
that if this moment isn't good enough
then no moment ever will be
that if you can't make peace with this moment
    now
then you'll always be at war.

It's time to stop trying
to bend the world to your will
to twist destiny to your own desires
but to allow life to unfold
with slow natural grace, like spring.

It's time to stop swimming
and let the river carry you.

Why strive so hard
when you can flow so easily?

When You Lose Yourself

When you find yourself wondering
how you're going to pass the time
and you scramble for arrangements
to fill the uneasy emptiness

When you find yourself wishing you were
        someone else
and stare enviously at the pages of magazines
wishing for better or more

When you catch yourself feeling that
        something's not quite right
but can't pin down what it is
and solitude feels unnerving
as if the room were filled with restless ghosts

When you catch your mind clinging to future
        dreams
looking forward to holidays a little too much
and you feel hungry for noise and activity
to immerse yourself in and forget —

It's only a sign that you've lost yourself
that there's a fog of worries and responsibilities
whirling through your mind

standing between you and the warmth and
    light
and spacious radiance of being.

It's only a sign that you've pushed yourself so
    hard
that you've dried up like a river in summer
and can't meet up with the ocean.

You don't need to do anything —
you need to do nothing
to lift yourself out of the noise and stress
until the fog has cleared
and your being has settled to stillness
and the connection forms itself again.

The Night Is Alive

I wake up to the diluted darkness
where only a few stars are strong enough
to penetrate the orange glow
that fills these gray geometric streets.

But the night is alive.
The space from the ground to the sky
is filled with a crackling electric haze —
particles spinning and clashing
as they weave in and out of existence.

The hissing of cosmic radiance
from the first millisecond of creation
and encompassing every moment since.
Every dispersed atom, swimming across this
    endless sea,
singing their original oneness.

The Wilderness

It takes courage to face up to reality —
it's so easy to live in avoidance
to lose yourself in a haze of diversion
in a lukewarm glow of entertainment
or a stream of never-ending activity
making sure you're always so immersed and
    occupied
that there's no time to wonder who you are.

It's so easy to hide behind beliefs
to find shelter behind layers of illusion
to lose yourself to a story
that seems to answer every question
and to fill every space where fear could grow.

It takes courage to stand naked and empty
without diversions or support
feeling the cold air of reality against your skin
surveying a seeming wilderness
asking yourself, "Where am I? What should I
    be doing here?"

But wait — stand firm, and soon you'll adjust.
This high altitude will inspire you
this cold air will refresh you
this silence will soothe you

this solitude will connect you to yourself
the emptiness you thought would turn you to
    stone
will welcome you home.

The wilderness is an oasis
and there is no need to escape.

The Mellow Glow

Why fight against the fading glow of youth?
Why try to freeze a process that can't be
  stopped?
You're clinging too hard, that's why you're
  weary;
your face is lined with tension, not with age.

And even if your form has altered a little
even if the surface is a little worn and chafed
your being is rich and deep
nourished by experience and understanding
and another kind of light is shining from you
  now:
a full, mellow glow, like autumn sunshine,
that spreads further and touches deeper
than the flashing, dazzling glow of youth.

Why not let that glow shine through
instead of trying to rekindle a faded light?

Change brings decay if you resist it.
But if you accept it and flow with it,
it brings growth and renewal.

The Fortress

You thought the idea was to accumulate
to colonize your inner space
and build yourself up, block by block,
until you were complete and impregnable
strong enough to stand up to the world.

But now you know you've been deceived —
so weighed down you can hardly move
so overcrowded with identity
that you've lost touch with your core
your boundaries so thick and solid
that your soul is suffocating.

But there's still time to declutter your soul.
Don't be sentimental — throw it all away.
Dismantle the fortress, block by block.
Break yourself down to nothing again —
become the emptiness you always were.

The Primal Soul

At first you were no one
a primal soul, an open space of being,
until they discovered you in the wilderness.

They took you to the city to civilize you
to build you an identity.
They taught you their signs and signals
gave you a religion and a nationality
and handed you a list of rules.
They showed you their ancient traditions
and told you it was your duty to maintain
    them.
They gave you a history and a destiny,
made you a character in their story.

They pointed out your brothers and sisters
told you that you were different and special
taught you to feel proud and loyal
and to be wary of those
with different rules and traditions
and different signs and signals
whose lives are less precious than yours.

And finally they were satisfied
that you belonged to them completely.

But it's not true — sometimes you feel it deep
    down inside
like the whisper of a faraway voice carried by
    the wind;
a faint memory of your primal state, and a
    longing to return.
You know the original open space of you is still
    there
underneath all those layers of identity —
indestructible, unchangeable.

And maybe now you're strong enough to
    reclaim yourself
maybe you're mature enough to become a child
    again.

So step out of the story —
exempt yourself from those ancient rules
cast off those old traditions
declare yourself free of the past and the future
with your own journey to discover
and your own reality to create.

Tell your people you're still one of them
just a member of a bigger group that they're all
    part of too —
a group with no rules or boundaries
that embraces without exclusion.

Tell your people there's too much at stake
for the human race to remain fragmented —
our broken pieces have already scarred the
    world too much.

Tell your people that you have new eyes
that can see the deep ocean of oneness
beneath the shifting surface waves.

Then walk back into the wilderness, naked and
    empty again,
and dance with primal joy.

The Same Substance

How can we be separate
when we're the same substance, body and soul,
collections of the same atoms
and channels of the same soul-force?

Let's be like children
whose beings are too empty
to be filled with distinctions
too open to be closed off by prejudice
too fluid to be clogged up with concepts —
so whole and so connected that they don't need
    to build
a fortress of identity.

What is it that separates us?
Only the illusion of identity —
only the illusion of separateness.

Death, the Mysterious Stranger

You know the mysterious stranger is coming to
    collect you.
You know you have an appointment but don't
    know when.
You see him around from time to time, taking
    care of his business
but you make sure you avoid his gaze, don't
    answer when he speaks.
There's so much you love here
so many people and places and pleasures you
    feel attached to
and so many goals left to achieve and ambitions
    to fulfill.
So why would you want to leave?
Maybe if you teach yourself to forget him
then he'll forget you too.

But avoidance only makes your fear grow
    stronger —
a fear too subtle to sense
like poisonous gas that slowly spreads through
    your being
tingeing your thoughts with anxiety.
A background dread of your own extinction

that makes every sound suspicious
every movement threatening and every
    moment a burden
while the mysterious stranger walks carefree,
nonchalant, scarcely aware of you.

Don't ignore him anymore —
turn to the stranger and embrace him, let him
    walk beside you,
and he'll reveal his true identity:
a magician who can transform your life
with the power of perspective and the magic of
    new meaning
who can turn listlessness to purpose
stone-cold hours to light-jeweled moments
a jaded old man's flatland to a child's new
    world of wonder.

And finally, when the mysterious stranger
    turns to you and nods,
you won't fight death but go willingly.
And as you walk across the border and enter
    his strange kingdom
where separateness and solidity melt away
and the softest clearest light engulfs you
and new dimensions unfold around you
flooding you with new knowledge (which you
    somehow always had) —

you smile serenely as you realize
that this kingdom is your home
and this journey will never end.

The Great Dictator

A shock of silence inside your mind
a sudden startling absence
of the ever-present chatter
and the ever-present pressure
and the ever-present ego —
    a crowded noisy auditorium
that's suddenly completely empty.

The crazy dictator who controlled your life
standing at your shoulder, judging and
    criticizing,
interfering with every impulse
distorting every situation
has mysteriously disappeared — at least for
    now.
His great palace is suddenly deserted
his ornate bed is empty and unmade
his lavish breakfast left half-eaten
his ministers have fled the country.

And the heavy humid atmosphere of
    oppression lifts
the air that bristled with mistrust and fear
breezes softly and lightly against your face
and your being, clenched tight like a fist,
relaxes and opens to free-flowing space.

And now you're free
to relish this strange stillness
that seeps beyond the boundaries of your self
this silence that is more than the absence of
    noise
this stillness that is more than the absence of
    activity —
a living silent stillness, a force field
swirling with subtle energies.

Perhaps the dictator will return to power
or another madman will replace him
but now that you've sensed the silence
now that you know how spacious and still you
    are
life will never be the same.

The dictator will never completely control you
    again;
a part of you will always be beyond his reach.
Freedom will always glimmer inside you.

The Gentle Sway of Death

(FOR IAN SMITH)

How could you disappear so suddenly
slipping away in the night without telling us
    your plans
leaving us here, bewildered,
staring numbly at the space you filled?

How should we accept
that there's no way of tracking you down
and bringing you back, to face your
    responsibilities?

How should we accept
that the sprawling mansion of your life
with all its secret passages and winding halls
and all the rooms you let us share
has vanished overnight with no trace left
almost as if it never stood?

But underneath the sadness there's a strange
    elation
a sympathetic joy.
I can sense a gentle sway
like the swell of water from a ship far away:
somewhere around me, invisible,

your consciousness is dissolving
your identity is slowly spreading
the single static point of you is melting
like ice into the ocean.

And I can sense your amazement
at this journey you never expected
your look of awestruck ecstasy
as you pass through
on your way to everything.

The Off-loading

Are you willing to give yourself up?
Are you ready to off-load your attachments
to relinquish your status and success
and allow your ambitions to fall away?
Are you prepared to step away
from this lifelong project of accumulation
and let your empire break apart?

One day you'll have to let go, willing or not,
so prepare yourself now, like a traveler
who knows she'll be leaving soon
and starts to cut her ties, hand over her duties,
and give away her possessions.

Then when the day of your departure comes
you won't cling to what you have to leave
    behind
your soul won't be racked with longing
or be weighed down by bitterness and regret.
Instead you'll be empty, peaceful, and light
and ready to float free.

The Trees

I swear the trees were speaking to me —
two great oaks hanging over the station wall
while the train was waiting
their leaves sparkling with deep rich green
their branches swaying softly.

They seemed like gurus, still and serene,
intersecting from an older world.
And they were saying, "Slow down —
don't strive for what's beyond your reach.
Don't chase the light so hard
that you lose your footing and uproot yourself.
Wait for the sun to come around to you."

They paused for a moment, then whispered,
"Don't let the future agitate your mind.
The present holds enough happiness for
      anyone.
Don't look forward, look around —
accept and be content."

The train whisked me away
soon we were hurtling down the track again
but my mind was completely motionless
standing still there with the trees.

I Am Eternally Grateful

"Now that you know what life is like
would you have chosen to be born?"
a pessimistic friend once asked.
He seemed surprised when I said, "Of course!"

I ponder the question again this morning
this ecstatic autumn morning
that fills me with right-ness and yes-ness
this morning of brilliant astral sunlight
that makes the whole world seem transparent
and this blue-beyond-perfection sky
with the smooth still purity of consciousness
    itself
and the foaming forming merging clouds
nuzzling and wrestling like new spring lambs.

Yes, I am grateful to have been born.
I am eternally grateful
for the gift of this brief life
to be a guest of time and space
hosted by this bountiful beautiful world
to taste the sweetness of substance
and the firmness of form and flesh.

I am eternally grateful
to be eternal
to never have been born
and to never die.

I Am One of the Free

(FOR MY ANCESTORS)

After centuries of darkness
I am in the light.
After centuries in prison
I have been released.

I am one of the free
the end of a long line of slaves
millworkers and miners
strangers to the daylight
sweating in the stale air
deafened by the rattle of looms
lungs filling up with cotton dust
shaking one another to stay awake
(because if they fell asleep they never woke up)
and shadows that stalked the underworld
suffocating slowly as they clawed the seams
in a darkness that sweltered with danger.

And before them, peasants and serfs
shivering and starving through winter
stooped over ploughs and scythes
chained to patches of their masters' soil
through endless stagnant centuries
rounded up like cattle by lords and kings

to fight for scraps of land
leaving their fields and families to rot.

Generations haunted by disease and death
traumatized by fear and loss
broken parents burying children
orphaned children numbed and scarred
defenseless against a brutal world.

A whole world of possibility
shrunken to a tiny dark circle of hell
souls like rivers, deep and rich,
shriveled to muddy pools.

Freedom isn't always easy —
too many choices can confuse you
too much open space can make you feel
    exposed
like soldiers at the end of a war
unnerved by silence and stillness —
you might feel guilty, that you don't deserve
    your freedom.

But what can we do but be grateful to them
for struggling through those centuries
to prize open this window of light?
And we can grow to deserve it by using it.

We owe it to them not to waste it
to never take it for granted
and always appreciate the fresh air and light
and the freedom to be instead of just to do
to stop and look and contemplate
and most of all, the freedom to become
to explore the depths that were closed to them
to release the potential that was dammed inside
    them
and let ourselves flow as fast and as far as we
    can
and try to illuminate the darkness
that still fills the lives of others.

The Play

Standing on the hillside on New Year's Eve
I watch the clouds crash and collide like waves
the full moon weaving in and out
showing her beautiful brilliant face
then covering it coyly again.

A pale-gray sky for a second
then an opening, and suddenly the clouds are
    glorious
as if a great Goddess is peering through
and flooding them with white radiance.
Then a giant door slams shut
and the light cuts out abruptly.

I feel as if I'm hiding behind some savannah
    bushes
watching a spectacular ritual
two animals playing an exotic game
hunting or mating, even both —
the play of the moon and clouds.

"How amazing to be a spectator of this scene,"
    I think.
Then suddenly distance collapses
my soul seems to melt and turn to liquid
to stretch and spread through space

until I'm hovering as high as the clouds
as wide as the spaces between them
even though I'm still rooted to the ground.

There's no need to look up
or even to look on
there's no one here to look
there are no spectators
There is only play.

Can You Be Happy with Nothing?

Can you be happy with nothing
without looking forward to happiness
without entertainments and activities
to distract you from unhappiness

without projects that excite you
with their promises of success
and that make you feel you're moving
closer and closer to happiness

without collecting more possessions
or climbing to higher status
and parading your wealth and prominence
to try to convince others — and yourself —
that you're happier than them?

If not, then your happiness is always on loan
secondhand and superficial
like a blanket that's quickly pulled away
leaving you cold and empty and craving more.

But you can be happy with nothing.
There's a happiness that has no cause
that doesn't come from consuming or
    collecting

and doesn't deceive or disappoint or quickly
    fade:
the well-being of being itself
that simply is — and is always there.

A deep rich glow of wholeness
a soft and subtle energy whose nature is bliss
like a steady-flowing river whose source is you.
A well-being you don't need to chase, only to
    uncover,
that you don't need to strive for, only allow.

Step Outside Yourself

You're not the center of the universe.

How can your problems be important
when there's an infinity of space around you
an eternity of time in front of you and behind
and seven billion other souls who share this
    struggle with you —
seven billion other centers
with their own perspectives and problems
at least as important as yours?

Step outside yourself.
Empty this cluttered room
and open the windows wide
so that the wind can blow through you.

Step aside and let yourself be taken over
by a force that's stronger than your suffering
a cause that lifts you up and carries you
high above this cramped reality
where this world of mental turmoil shrinks
    almost to nothing
while your being spreads and stretches,
    becoming everything,

until you're no longer the center of the
   universe
but a flowing expression of the whole.

The World Is Reborn

The world is reborn every moment
rising out of nothing like a miracle
new created, fresh, unnamed,
gleaming with strange beauty.

A world without time, untouched by thought,
not yet carved or labeled
or neutered by concepts and categories —
just raw unfiltered is-ness.

It's only our minds that make the world old
adding on our habits and memories
attaching our stale assumptions —
until time itself is tired
and each day sags with boredom.

But in the rebirth of the world, we're reborn
    too —
every moment is a new beginning
an amnesty from the past
a chance to re-create ourselves
to shake ourselves free of limitations
and explore this bright new world.

The Beginning of the Universe

When two lovers come together
and two cells meet and merge
there's a miniature big bang
and a universe begins.

It may seem inconsequential —
two strangers seeking pleasure
a drunken fling or favor
a jaded housewife's weekly chore

but really they're two gods
creating a new reality
an awesome responsibility
a world to nurture and oversee.

Gases solidify and atoms collect
consciousness spreads through the radiant void
and slowly the universe takes form and shape
expanding and slowly settling.

Every universe is an experiment
a new web of planets and galaxies
weaving new patterns and possibilities
creating new laws of nature.

Every universe is an adventure
a voyage through uncharted time and space
tentative steps forward and trailblazing paths
colliding and intersecting.

And every universe is a mystery
filled with hidden fissures and tunnels
teeming with invisible energies
and infinite, dark potentials.

And almost as soon as the expansion slows
the slow movement of entropy begins
the connections weaken and the fragments
    spread
until the whole organism crumbles and
    collapses.

A slow decay or a giant crunch
and again the stillness of the void.

The Trees (2)

It's so soothing to walk among the trees
on paths knotted with their roots
and blanketed with their leaves
to feel them charging the air with ease —
it feels like floating in a pool of deep rich green.

But I feel a tinge of sadness too —
once the world belonged to trees.
We were only their guests, as I am now,
walking in their shadows
sucking like babies at their fruit.
We only saw the sky through their branches.
Tender mothers, the source of life —
why did we need gods when we could worship
    trees?

But then we grew hungry for autonomy
and rejected their easy fruit.
We stepped out of the shadows and cleared a
    space
to grind our crops out of the ground.
Jealous of their effortless dominion
we slashed and burned them down
like Columbus tearing through the New World
amazed at how easily they fell at our feet.

And now we think the earth is ours.
These trees don't seem to care —
the sadness is mine, not theirs.
They have time, they're content to wait,
until we realize that autonomy is an illusion
that identity can't survive without being shared;
until we remember that we're still their guests —
or don't remember and leave the world to them
	again —
a broken world that will heal in time
back into primal harmony.

The Unease

How can you allow yourself to be happy
when you know that something's not quite right?

There's a sense of unease that's hard to define —
as if you're being watched
even though you're at home alone
as if someone's been through your belongings
although nothing seems out of place.

A sense of incompletion —
an appointment you must have forgotten
a job you didn't finish
or a debt you forgot to repay
even though you've checked and checked again
and your affairs all seem in order.

But look again — there's nothing wrong.
Everything is just as it should be.
There's nothing to be wary of, no problems
    to fix.
You're completely safe and free.

Look inside yourself, that's the source of your
    unease —
your agitated mind, with its crazy spinning
    thoughts,

claustrophobic like a tiny crowded bar
where you're trapped between the tables
listening to a hundred different conversations.

Slow down and be still for a moment
until your mind begins to settle
and the air begins to clear
and the walls begin to soften
and feel how your agitation begins to fade
and how ease begins to fill you
like fresh air through an open window.

Feel how peaceful the world is
and how easy life can be.

Then give yourself permission to be content.

The Meaning

You can't explain the meaning
reduce it to thought or confine it to words
break it down to basic building blocks
or trace it back to an origin.

But when you see the meaning, you know it.
Just when you've forgotten it existed
you're driving along the highway
and you turn your head to the side
as if someone's tapped your shoulder
and it's there, stretched across the evening sky
filling the spaces between the clouds.

You open the door to empty the trash
and it's there, rustling with the wind through
    the trees,
stroking your face softly like a lover.
You tilt your head back to catch the rain
and it's there, falling with the infinite silver
    points,
bringing down benevolence from the sky.

Your eyes spring open in the middle of the
    night
as if there's an intruder, an unfamiliar noise,

and it's there — in the dense rich darkness that
    fills the room
and the glow of unconscious communion
that envelops you and your partner.

The most familiar forgotten place
your home from a previous lifetime.
A mother's soothing presence
and her warm enfolding arms.

The Strangeness

Don't let the world become familiar —
don't forget the sheer strangeness of being
    alive.

Don't forget the sheer strangeness of being
    here
on the surface of this spinning globe
standing in its soft dark soil, immersed in
    atmospheric gases,
with the blue-tinted sky above, full of foaming
    crystal masses,
turning to face a burning golden ball
that caresses us with heat and light
until the blue fades to black as it opens up
to the vast empty fullness of the universe.

Don't forget the sheer strangeness of being this
    body
that breathes and blinks and heals and grows
a miracle of precision and complexity
a city of ceaseless traffic and industry
where a million microscopic processes
    intertwine
and millions of tiny organisms labor
for the greater good of you
just to keep you conscious and alive.

Don't forget the strangeness of seeming to be a
    ghostly self
that lives inside your body, that has attached
    itself to your form,
that seems to stare out from your eyes
and can spin webs of logic, create alternate
    abstract worlds,
and turn into itself and expand into
endless spacious consciousness.

Don't forget the sheer strangeness of this
    world of form
where matter pulses with consciousness
and shimmers with waves of light
into infinite expressions and variations
of the same rich source, the same elemental
    theme,
the same essential sound in different
    frequencies
this roaring teeming swell of life
the brightness and shining nakedness of now
and awe-inspiring is-ness of the nameless real.

A strangeness even stranger
because it's not hostile or indifferent
but right and reassuring, somehow warm and
    welcoming,
like a chaos that was always planned
a riddle that makes perfect sense

a cacophony of meaning, full of hidden
   harmony —
glorious harmonious strangeness.

The Force

Four o'clock in the morning
pacing about the room
trying to coax our baby back to sleep
I look over to the window —
a square of pure primeval darkness
between the half-drawn curtains
millions of years old
millions of miles deep.
A pocket of the universe
a tunnel into space
black, cold, and silent
but alive.

The force flows through the window
thick and viscous
but at the same time subtle and vapor thin
enveloping and entering me
like smoke, foaming through my body
slow and heavy, merging and becoming me.

Inside me there's only darkness —
awesome and immense, almost frightening,
but glowing with warm benevolence.

The Perfect Paradox

When you can hear silence behind the noise
and feel space among the crowd
when you can sense peace amid chaos and
    conflict
and see the beauty of the ugly and drab

When solitude never leads to loneliness
and emptiness seems to overflow
when every stranger looks familiar
and every foreign place feels like home

Then you'll know that duality is no more
that you've stepped beyond contradiction
into the place of perfect paradox
where everything makes sense.

The End of Success

There's no success now — your chance has
    passed.
The judge looked over your case again but still
    shook her head
and now your failure's too final ever to be
    reversed.

They told you to never give up, but it's too
    late —
if you keep trying to move forward you'll just
    sink even deeper.

But now that there's no way forward
this is your chance to stop and look around.
Watch as the road behind you vanishes
and a landscape begins to emerge, as if through
    morning fog —
a brilliant panorama, fresh and lush with
    meaning,
with no direction anywhere, only depth and
    space.
It was always here but you never saw it —
because you were never here.

And finally it's clear
that fulfillment isn't a place to seek

but the place from which you're seeking
that wholeness isn't a distant future goal
but your closest present state
that no matter how much success you
    accumulate
or how much failure trails behind you
it's always enough to be alive.

The End of Desire

If what you want is endless pleasure, wealth, or
    fame,
then you will always want.
You will never reach a place of peace.

A few moments of respite
while you digest the experience
then the same restless hunger
the gnawing incompleteness
only a little more powerful and rarefied
because your palette is a little more refined
and your sense of taste a little more dulled.

Desire is like a fertilized cell
that forever splits and multiplies
and never reaches a final form
only disperses and dilutes your mind
and takes you even further away from the
    source.

You might think you've reached the end of
    desire
but then the mist clears
and you realize this peak is only a plateau
the bottom of an even higher peak.

The harder you search for happiness
turning the world upside down
for a legendary treasure that was never there
the more you lose touch with the shining
    source
of peace and joy inside you.

Don't desire anything
except the end of desire.

Savor This World, Savor This Life

Savor this world
because your ship only landed here by chance
on the shore of this strange island
in the middle of an empty ocean
and you can only stay here for a while
wandering these lush forests
eating these exotic fruits
until your ship sets sail again.

Savor this world
because you're only a guest passing through
   this town
stopping off to visit some relatives on your
   way back home
not long enough to put down any roots
walking these foreign streets
nodding at passers-by — the locals, you
   presume.
But look more closely — everyone's a traveler
   here.

Savor this life
because it's passing away like a fast-flowing
   river
and there's nothing to hold on to
no branches overhead to grasp

no bushes by your side to catch —
nothing to do but to swim with the flow
and lose yourself
in the roar and the rhythm and the rush.

Savor this life
because you've won the greatest prize
the freedom of the city
the keys to the kingdom
a lifelong cruise through time and space
the honor of experience
the accolade of existence.
And one day you'll have to give it back.

And when that day comes you won't feel any
    bitterness
only gratitude for the privilege of being
as long you have lived in celebration
as long you have lived in appreciation
as long as you have savored the world.

The Project

There's more to this than you realize.
You're part of a project that's too vast for you
    to comprehend.
The impulses that guide your life
don't come from you, but through you —
you're a channel, not the source.

But the impulses aren't flowing through you
    clearly —
you've let the channel become obstructed
by your self-doubt and fear.
So the force has been diluted, the message has
    been distorted,
and the river that should be rushing through
    you
is a halting, stuttering stream.

But this project is too important to interfere
    with.
There's too much at stake to stand in its
    way —
to be distracted by your own fears and desires
to be afraid of failure or wary of success
to worry about looking foolish or losing face
to wonder who's watching you and what they
    might be thinking

and be discouraged if no one seems to be
    watching at all
or frustrated if they don't seem to understand.

It's enough to do what you're meant to do
to express what you're meant to express
without evaluating your effect
or considering results or reactions.

There's too much at stake for you to become
anything less than you were meant to be,
to leave the smallest part of your potential
    unfulfilled
or the smallest piece of your message unsaid.

This is the time to be fearless
so that the force can flow through you freely.
This is the time to be empty
so that the source can fill you completely.
This is the time to step aside
and let the project unfold through you.

Back Home

Back home
to the place where the sky is as wide as space
where the clouds caress one another as they
    float
where the trees are dancing messengers of the
    wind
where shapes are clear and fine and colors seem
    to shine
as if they're cut from the clearest glass.

Back home
to the soothing serene energy of the self
the underground river that makes the soil so
    rich
with roots stretching way, way down
into the safe and sturdy ground
so that stress and fear can't bend or break you.

Back home
to the place where time opens up, almost seems
    to stop,
and there's no more striving or seeking or even
    doing
only a graceful glide of being through every
    easy day

and the pressure of the future fades away
like an army retreating
leaving the present in peace.

The Essence

The essence of you is emptiness
the essence of you is love
the essence of you is energy
the essence of you is bliss.

The essence of you flows like a fountain
from a pool of pure consciousness at the heart
   of reality.
The essence of you surges with an eternal force
that has borrowed you for this lifetime.

The essence of you is deathless.
This form will wither and dissolve away
then the essence will return to its source
to find a new expression.

The essence of you stretches
inside and outside your body
inside and outside time
within and beyond the world
at home, in peace, in every place.

Acknowledgments

I would like to express my gratitude to Eckhart Tolle, Kim Eng, and Marc Allen for their support and enthusiasm for this book. Heartfelt thanks to Susan Miller for her many helpful suggestions and comments. Thanks also to Jonathan Wichmann for many other helpful editorial suggestions. Finally, many thanks to O Books, for allowing us to include several pieces previously published in my book *The Meaning*.

Index of First Lines

About the Author

Steve Taylor is the author of several books on spirituality and psychology, including *The Fall* and *Waking from Sleep*. He has also published a previous book of poetic spiritual reflections, *The Meaning*. He is a senior lecturer in psychology at Leeds Beckett University in the United Kingdom. Since 2011, he has appeared annually in *Mind, Body, Spirit* magazine's list of "the world's 100 most spiritually influential living people." Visit his website at www.stevenmtaylor.com.

About Eckhart Tolle Editions

Eckhart Tolle Editions was launched in 2015 to publish life-changing works, both old and new, that have been personally selected by Eckhart Tolle. This imprint of New World Library presents books that can powerfully aid in transforming consciousness and awakening readers to a life of purpose and presence.

Learn more about Eckhart Tolle at

www.eckharttolle.com

NEW WORLD LIBRARY is dedicated to publishing books and other media that inspire and challenge us to improve the quality of our lives and the world.

We are a socially and environmentally aware company. We recognize that we have an ethical responsibility to our customers, our staff members, and our planet.

We serve our customers by creating the finest publications possible on personal growth, creativity, spirituality, wellness, and other areas of emerging importance. We serve New World Library employees with generous benefits, significant profit sharing, and constant encouragement to pursue their most expansive dreams.

As a member of the Green Press Initiative, we print an increasing number of books with soy-based ink on 100 percent postconsumer-waste recycled paper. Also, we power our offices with solar energy and contribute to non-profit organizations working to make the world a better place for us all.

Our products are available in bookstores everywhere.

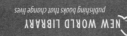

www.newworldlibrary.com

At NewWorldLibrary.com you can download our catalog,
subscribe to our e-newsletter, read our blog,
and link to authors' websites, videos, and podcasts.

Find us on Facebook, follow us on Twitter, and watch us on YouTube.

Send your questions and comments our way!
You make it possible for us to do what we love to do.

Phone: 415-884-2100 or 800-972-6657
Catalog requests: Ext. 10 | Orders: Ext. 52 | Fax: 415-884-2199
escort@newworldlibrary.com

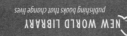

NEW WORLD LIBRARY
publishing books that change lives   14 Pamaron Way, Novato, CA 94949